CHAKRA AFFIRMATIONS

300 AFFIRMATIONS ENERGETICALLY TAILORED FOR
CLEARING, HEALING, AND BALANCING THE SEVEN
MAJOR CHAKRAS

ASA KELSANG

CONTENTS

Introduction   5

AFFIRMATIONS
First, Root Chakra   15
Second, Sacral Chakra   21
Third, Solar Plexus Chakra   29
Fourth, Heart Chakra   35
Fifth, Throat Chakra   41
Sixth, Third Eye Chakra   47
Seventh, Crown Chakra   55
Closing Affirmations   61

Conclusion   63

INTRODUCTION

Hi there,

Welcome to Chakra Affirmations! This book was designed as a potent tool to clear, heal, and balance your chakras through the use of affirmations. The affirmations contained are energetically designed to target specific areas of challenge within each chakra, and return them to optimal working condition.

Meaning "wheel" in Sanskrit, our chakras are a vital component of our broader energy system. While the discussion of chakras is a fresh topic in modern spirituality, the concept is arguably as old as spirituality itself, made more widely known through both Hindu and Buddhist religious traditions. Much like maintaining a healthy body through diet and exercise, the clearing and balancing of our chakras is equally critical for our emotional, mental, and energetic health.

The first, or root chakra governs issues related to personal safety, security, and groundedness in the physical plane. It is located at the end of your tailbone, near your perineum. A healthy root chakra means you're cultivating a strong sense of security and safety in your daily life, and are comfortable with expressing yourself physically.

Your second, or sacral chakra, is responsible for your emotional, sensual, and creative expressions. If your sacral chakra is balanced and clear, you are exercising a healthy sensuality, and are channeling your emotions and feelings into the world in a balanced and constructive way.

The third, or solar plexus chakra, concerns issues of personal empowerment, individual willpower and autonomy. You are able to assert yourself ethically, and affect greater change in the outer world with a healthy and balanced solar plexus.

The fourth chakra, also known as the heart chakra, is somewhat self explanatory. The heart chakra governs issues of interpersonal love, self love, and global compassion. If your heart chakra is healthy, you are relating to the world from a place of kindness and benevolence, able to forgive yourself and those around you for past transgressions.

The fifth chakra, or the throat chakra concerns issues of self expression and communication. A healthy throat chakra means you are able to express yourself and your ideas accurately, communicating your inner truth without difficulty.

The sixth, or third eye chakra, governs dimensions of inner vision, psychic input, discernment and insight. With a healthy third eye you are able to successfully apply and follow your intuition, and perceive insightful and creative solutions to both inner and outer problems.

The seventh, or crown chakra, involves the integration and embodiment of broader spiritual wisdom, universal truth and knowledge, and higher spiritual perspectives. A healthy crown chakra means you are incorporating higher wisdom into your everyday words and actions, setting an example for the world around you perhaps as a healer, or teacher.

While there are more chakras associated with your energy system than the seven listed above, these seven are the primary which dictate most aspects of your everyday life.

While it is recommended to clear and balance each chakra in progressive fashion, if you feel that one is in greater need of healing than the rest, it's okay to focus on that specific chakra and bring it back into balance. If we have the time, or suspect that more than one chakra needs balancing, it's ideal to work progressively through each chakra to ensure a holistic healing has taken place, but it's okay to bounce around depending on what works best for you.

Having a balanced, healthy, and operating chakra system accounts for the quality of our emotional experience in life. When our chakras are balanced, happiness, relief, and joy are more easily attained and shared. With these feelings, our physical bodies are then more easily supported, motivating us to seek activities that we enjoy and that enhance our overall well being.

While the chakras can naturally balance themselves through holistic, healthy lifestyle practices, it's harder to maintain an ideal condition without conscious practice. A given chakra can become closed, damaged, or clouded from a variety of experiences in life, without the individual even being aware that it's happened. Because of this, directly targeting these energy centers with constructive, healing intent is an effective, alchemical approach to prevent yourself from falling further into damaging behaviors and thought patterns.

Each affirmation in this book contains a unique geometry of intention, which when expressed, captures an aspect of experience relevant to a given chakra. By speaking the affirmation aloud, or reading with silent intent, the underlying chakra is not only cleared, but healed and brought into balance with its adjacent energy centers.

Each chapter advances from one chakra to the next, starting with the root, moving through the crown.

When reading, it is important for you to sustain the intent of the words as you progress through each affirmation. By holding the intent of the words read, the healing potential behind the affirmations will have a deeper and longer lasting effect. While reading to yourself without speaking is acceptable, it is also encouraged to read the affirmations aloud. By speaking each affirmation out loud, it verbally asserts their intent, further solidifying their truth in your physical environment.

As you read, if one affirmation feels more resonant than another for you, feel free to recite or repeat it until the energy surrounding it is resolved enough to move on. You may also write down or journal your progress, assign certain chakra affirmations to different days of the week, or cherry pick your favorites to recite on specific occasions. In healing, it's important to follow what feels right to you. While reading each affirmation with emotional intent is ideal, there are truly no strict rules in this process.

With that said, you are encouraged to revisit each chapter whenever it feels appropriate. In reading, allow for whatever experience comes up to move through you, without fear, judgement, or attachment. As you'll experience more directly in the first chapter, it is important to focus on your grounding, acknowledging that the life systems of this planet are invested in your wellbeing.

The process of healing chakras is as much about releasing old trauma, as it is about correcting a broken system of energetic function. Each chakra responds to your emotions and experiences, negative and positive, and can become stuck with latent programming from traumatic events. If uncomfortable memories or feelings do arise, welcome those feelings with an open heart to be processed and released, and know you wouldn't be experiencing them if you weren't also able to heal and release them.

Hold compassion for yourself as you heal, understanding that there is a more complete version of yourself waiting on the other side!

If you feel the chakra of a given chapter is already balanced, feel free to move on to the next and begin balancing chakra in the following chapter.

Thank you for reading, and I send you with light and support on your journey of growth, reintegration, and healing!

AFFIRMATIONS

FIRST, ROOT CHAKRA

I am fundamentally safe and supported in my life.

I am powerful, strong, and well founded in my body.

I am deserving of a safe, balanced, and secure lifestyle.

I am loved, appreciated, and acknowledged even by people who I have never met.

I am willing to receive increased emotional and financial security in my life.

I am an abundant, deserving being.

I am feeling grounded, protected, and present in my body.

I can feel myself becoming ready to grow into new areas of my experience.

I am a co-creator of the universe and I trust that all my needs can and will be met.

I am grounded into the earth, and am securely held in this place throughout my day.

Even if I don't see them, I have access to all the resources I need at any given time, and I am grateful to my experience for ensuring this fact.

Through grounding, I am more mentally and emotionally balanced, and by healing my root chakra, I find grounding more easily.

I feel into the gravity holding my feet and body to the ground, and invite my root chakra to forge a stronger connection to the earth through this sensation.

Even in circumstances without modern amenities, I can find ways to take care of myself, in order to survive.

I am deserving of love, appreciation, and acknowledgement for my unique needs and for the individual I am.

The universe conspires to meet my needs in ways that are appropriate for my current level of growth.

I am grateful for the security that already exists in my life, because in being grateful for my security, more will be created.

The universe creates as much time and space as I need in order for me to move, and grow through difficult passages.

I receive intuitive input regarding foods that will help balance my body and energy system, starting with my root chakra.

At any given time, my body knows exactly what foods it needs to heal itself, and I will listen more closely for it to give me those signals.

At any given time, there are multiple avenues of prosperity available to me to support my life and my goals.

My experience continually seeks to enhance my financial security, and I am open to noticing these opportunities when they arise.

Physical movement and play are important in maintaining a healthy physical condition, which also heals and strengthens my root chakra.

I am open to finding approaches of exercise and athletic expression that are both fun and fulfilling for my body.

I am open to the universe for creating an increased state of protection and safety in my daily experience.

I can feel and visualize my root chakra rotating at a healthy diameter, synchronized with my broader system.

I take pleasure in observing the natural world, and look forward to noticing beautiful and interesting details in nature.

I am fundamentally lovable for who I am, and I deserve to be cared for by others.

I am enough, and I am good enough.

The fact that I am still here is evidence that I am actually good enough.

Areas of my life where I feel insecure, or not good enough in some way, are simply parts of myself that need to heal, and they will be healed.

I am grounded and connected to the earth at all times, my welfare is a top priority in the evolution of the planet.

There are places in nature that feel more like home to me than others, and I know I can always return to these places to be healed and reoriented on my path.

At any moment I am never truly lost, and I only need to remember this fact when I feel scared or out of place.

I am an abundant, attractive being and my reality playfully awaits my engagement with it.

I am powerfully connected to the earth beneath me, and I am capable of repairing this connection when I sense that it is lost.

I am grateful for my ability to rebalance and heal my body, and my root chakra at any time.

The systems of the earth support my well being, and are capable of nourishing me when I ask them too.

I am continually able to create safety and security by myself, and I only need to look inward to achieve this.

Feelings of safety and security are a natural state of being, and my system is continually pursuing a return to this state, even without my awareness.

My body, and overall being is a self-healing, self correcting system, and is continually finding ways to heal and repair itself to an optimum state of health.

I will listen to my body when something does or doesn't sound good, and will honor those feelings next time they are encountered.

I look forward to cultivating more calming, peaceful, and relaxing experiences in my life.

Inner peace is a true state of wealth, and I look forward to acquainting myself with this feeling more regularly.

SECOND, SACRAL CHAKRA

I am grateful for my ability to feel.

I deserve to feel my emotions, and to have them expressed.

I am grateful for my emotions, as they provide greater context for growth and learning from life.

I am grateful for my sensuality.

It is safe for me to express my creative nature.

I am a creative spirit who enjoys finding inspiration through experiencing their emotions.

I am becoming comfortable with my own sexuality, and the ways it seeks expression in respect to the boundaries of others.

I recognize that whatever urges which seem difficult to control are created from a reservoir of emotion waiting to be felt, and I am open to feeling these emotions at whatever pace is right for me.

I am open to removing any notions of guilt around my sexuality, as sexuality is a central experience of life.

I create healthy boundaries with myself and others, and stand confidently in my own personal space.

I accept all of my feelings, even if some are difficult to reason with.

I know that by feeling into my emotions, even difficult ones, without identifying with them, I can more easily integrate and release them.

There is no reason for me to feel shame for myself or who I am.

Pleasure is an integral aspect of life, and I welcome the opportunity to experience it without guilt or shame.

I enjoy experiencing my emotions, and make sure to create time and space for them to be felt.

I am grateful for my ability to experience my feelings, and know that my emotions represent parts of myself that are grateful for being heard.

My emotions are sacred, and are expressions of truth from my inner self that are always worth listening to.

The acknowledgement of my feelings is equally important to anyone else's, and they have the right to be expressed and heard.

I am open to finding expansive forms of creative expression that will serve my broader nature.

The forms in which my emotions and feelings seek expression are sacred, and I lovingly accept and release whatever pain or shame I carry around them.

I enjoy many forms of sensuality, and I am genuinely grateful for the experience of having a body.

I compassionately release any toxic obligations I hold towards others that do not serve my greater well-being.

Sometimes, it's easy to confuse someone else's feelings with my own, and I ask my higher power to remove whatever energy I am carrying that doesn't belong to me.

In caring for others, it's easy to forget my own needs, and I commit to taking care of myself even if it feels somewhat selfish.

I believe in the value of establishing healthy boundaries, and I seek to resolve any personal boundary issues present in my life.

I will prioritize creating healthy boundaries with people in my life who are overly demanding, and will work to keep my own energy in a healthy state of balance.

I value the relationships with people I have in my life, even the difficult ones, because they provide contrast for me to better understand myself.

I look forward to cultivating healthy relationships in my life, and welcome new opportunities to define what this experience means for me.

It is my birthright to experience joy and excitement, and I use these feelings as vibratory signals for where I want to take my life.

I allow emotions which are ready to be felt to flow freely into my consciousness, and I observe without judgement the origin of each feeling to extract the lesson behind it.

I take joy in experiencing my feelings, as they help tell my story and clarify what I want from my experience.

It's important to discern between emotions and sensations, and both are equally relevant in my life.

I recognize that sexual energy is also creative energy, and I can choose how I want this energy to be expressed.

I am comfortable with channeling my feelings into tangible, creative outlets.

I love the prospect of creating something that not only helps me, but the world around me.

Blocking emotions, like the flow of a stream, cause

imbalances in the greater system, and I am willing to let my emotions flow by listening to them without judgement.

There are simple pleasures in life which hold importance for me, and I commit to pursuing them more regularly.

I respect my feelings as something as important to listen to as hunger or thirst.

I welcome all feelings — big, scattered, and old — to be felt in a space of unconditional love to be heard and released to the universe.

I acknowledge that there are higher sensory experiences in life that can be felt when I'm in balance, and I look forward to having these experiences more often.

I feel healthy and safe to be myself, without fear of victimization or persecution for the way I feel.

I can feel my sacral chakra now rotating at a healthy diameter, integrating with my root chakra.

My sacral chakra is supportively engaging my broader chakra system, and the strength of my personal energy is expanding as a result.

THIRD, SOLAR PLEXUS CHAKRA

I own my personal space, and choose to stand confidently in my personal power.

I have the right to express my autonomy without deferring to someone else's preference.

I deserve to experience my personal power in life, and I'm open to how this power wishes to express itself.

In being assertive with my sense of self, I don't need to apologize for who I am.

I release whatever obstacles or assumptions that are held over me which block the flow of my own personal power.

In past situations where I didn't stand up for myself or my beliefs, I can go back and picture myself in my power, defending what I stand for.

I can act from a place of confidence and autonomy while still holding compassion for others.

Healing is as much about letting in my personal power as it is being willing to heal, and I am open to letting in my power to support my healing.

Compassion and accommodation are not the same thing, and I am willing to draw the line when I'm feeling taken advantage of.

I am ready to stand up for myself and my feelings more frequently.

I recognize that there are others who would seek to block my light and power, and I am unafraid to challenge them.

In understanding the influence others have in my life, I can choose to take greater control of my own life, and my future.

I stand up for myself, and don't let others walk over me

or allow them to compromise my personal sovereignty or sense of autonomy.

Protecting my personal power ensures my mental and spiritual well-being.

My personal power is something I can, and do, generate on my own without needing approval from anyone.

I am grateful for the inextinguishable power that is gifted to me, and my gratitude only expands the quality of this energy.

This power comes from an inexhaustible reservoir inside me, and while my physical body may become tired from channeling it, this energy is in infinite supply.

I recognize that this power from within represents the strength of my spirit in its purest form, and this energy is indestructible.

It has been from places of personal power that the most impactful societal inventions and movements were created, and I am ready to embody how this energy might express itself through me.

My inexhaustible reservoir of power is charged by my unique identity signature, and when I share this energy, it positively radiates to those around me.

Others recognize what I stand for when I act from my true identity, and I look to stand in this energy more regularly.

I am stable, powerful, and justified in being my genuine self.

I act from a space of compassion, and all actions I take include the consideration for the welfare of others.

The outside world is primed to receive the scope of my personal power, and I am ready and excited to share it with discretion.

The personal power I carry might make others uncomfortable, but I am ready to embody it without apologizing.

I forgive myself for times in my past when I acted from my power with negative intent, and send healing to those who my actions negatively affected.

I congratulate myself for my personal achievements, and take pride in every victory in life I've had so far.

I deserve to feel good about myself.

I recognize the importance of maintaining benevolent intent when acting from a place of personal power.

Ultimately, I am a fundamentally benevolent being, and I allow the knowledge of that fact to guide my power, and action in life.

I strive for a measure of consideration with each action I take, because acting without forethought can lead to harming myself or others.

I act with a keen sense of my surroundings, and for the motivations of those in my circles.

My self confidence doesn't come from the need to prove myself in any specific way, but from my induplicable uniqueness.

The power I radiate from the center of my being helps others find their own sense of power, creating a chain reaction of self empowerment in my social circle.

I am excited at the prospect of helping others find their own sense of personal empowerment.

I can feel my solar plexus chakra expand radiantly around me, and in this space I can confidently act in the direction of my highest truths.

I am willing to take on the responsibility of sharing my personal power with the world.

I bask in the fortifying radiance that emanates from my solar plexus, and visualize it filling the space surrounding my physical body.

This enhanced rate of spin increases the radius of my solar plexus chakra, allowing more of my personal light and power to shine through.

I envision my solar plexus chakra beginning to rotate faster in order to shed any toxic, foreign energies that would seek to undermine my state of well-being.

FOURTH, HEART CHAKRA

I am worthy of unconditional love.

I am fundamentally lovable for my personality and what I have to offer the world.

To the extent I am comfortable with it, I seek to share my love with the world.

When I am quiet, my soul communicates with me as a quiet voice in my heart, and I'm grateful to have this capacity.

I let go of all resentment towards myself, and forgive myself for negative perceptions I've held about myself since I was young.

I compassionately project love towards myself, and toward the wounds I've endured.

I forgive myself for mistakes I've made that have hurt myself and others, knowing that I deserve to be forgiven, even my inner critic.

I include all of my transgressions in a healing arch that extends backward into my past, acknowledging the pain I've caused and extending healing while forgiving myself for my actions.

In forgiving myself for my past actions, I let the guilt and remorse for what I've done flow through and out of my system, retaining the lesson of each experience.

While I might not yet be able to forgive those who have harmed me, I acknowledge the possibility that the harm they caused was created from a wound inside them that isn't reflective of their true self.

Love is a radical force, and I am open to how this force might demonstrate itself to me in my life.

I am bigger than my wounds, trauma, and anxiety, and I am transmuting the pain of each of these challenges with self compassion on a daily basis.

Being myself is a critical aspect of life, and I enjoy filling my environment with my presence.

I wouldn't be reading these words if I didn't have the capacity and desire to heal myself.

I am inherently loveable for who I am, and I am grateful for the person I get to be.

Not only am I loveable, I am likeable for the person I am, and I am appreciated by those in my everyday experience.

I understand that I have endured much, and hold only appreciation and gratitude for my endurance through the difficult experiences I've encountered.

I willingly radiate love to people in my life as an act of unconditional love, and remain open to how the universe returns this energy to me in exchange.

I am grateful for the love that is abundantly available to me at any given moment.

I know in my heart that I am adored for who I am, and I am grateful for this fact.

I endeavor to help others not because of what I might get in return, but because I truly care for the well being of others.

The sense of love I have for others transcends those in my immediate life, and I intentionally project my love to those anywhere who are open to receiving this energy.

I visualize complete strangers receiving the surplus of unconditional love I have, and feel their emotional state lifting.

I send love and gratitude to my family, friends, and those who have supported me throughout my life.

I send love even to those who I find difficult or challenging, as they are likely struggling in their own way.

I seek to include all of my perceived enemies in a bubble of my healing intent, letting them know that on a fundamental level, I support the love that exists within them.

The feeling of being seen and appreciated for the unique person I am is an increasingly common experience for me.

There are people in my life who rejoice in me being myself around them.

I am acknowledged in more than one way for the specific qualities I bring to the world.

I am grateful for my ability to exchange unconditional love as a constructive energy, and appreciate the different ways this energy is reciprocated.

My sense of unconditional love broadens to include all life forms on our planet, and ultimately the whole of the planet itself.

I feel the earth receiving my unconditional love, and it subtly reciprocates through my heart.

I endeavor to be in my heart space more often, and to see the world less from a place of right and wrong, and more from a place of healing and forgiveness.

I realize that central to unconditional love is forgiveness, and I extend the intent to forgive to anyone who genuinely seeks it.

I understand that healing is needed on the planet now more than ever, and I understand that by healing myself, I am able to help heal others who are going through similar challenges.

I welcome my higher guidance to lead me to opportunities to provide healing for others, myself, and the planet.

There are more opportunities than I realize to help others by being kind, and I invite my higher guides to help align me to those opportunities.

There is no greater power than love, and I welcome the strength of that energy through my heart chakra, and into my present experience.

My heart chakra is now radiating outwards expansively in my energy field, expelling lingering negative thoughtforms and energy.

My heart chakra welcomes and integrates the lower chakras into its rotation, and continues to actively heal both my physical and energy body.

FIFTH, THROAT CHAKRA

My truth is worth expressing, and others appreciate what I have to share.

I deserve to express myself, even if some aren't ready to listen.

I enjoy sharing my individuality with the world, and I am grateful for each opportunity to do so.

I am grateful for my ability and capacity to express myself.

I find enjoyment in creating and expressing myself in aesthetically unique ways.

I find enjoyment in communicating and expressing my individuality.

I release all negativity and fear that prevents me from speaking my truth.

Even if I feel uncomfortable vocalizing or sharing my truth, I know that it is fundamentally acceptable for me to do so.

I enjoy formulating articulate sentences, and take time to make sure my thoughts are verbalized coherently.

I express myself with ease and authenticity.

I love sharing ideas that are valuable to others, and helping other people gain greater understanding around an issue.

Expressing myself authentically is liberating, and I endeavor to create this experience more frequently.

My opinions are valid, and are healthy to be shared.

There are certain songs I enjoy listening to and singing along with, even if just to myself.

I recognize that through talking I am able to bring healing to others, and I appreciate this quality of my communication.

Even if I don't do so with words, I can responsibly communicate my mood to others with non verbals or body language.

I recognize an upwelling of energy in my throat, and welcome this energy to find an expressive outlet through me in whatever expression feels right.

Self expression is a foundational tool for preserving mental health, and I value opportunities to process emotion through expressing myself.

Even if I don't have a large audience, I can find creative ways of expressing myself with my work, or in my lifestyle choices.

How one lives their life is an act of expression, and I enjoy imagining new ways of communicating my individuality.

Through observing how others express themselves, I find inspiration for ways of better expressing myself and my ideas.

I appreciate humor that is both witty and intellectual, or silly and absurd.

Enjoying and sharing humor isn't frivolous or impractical, but critical for emotional health.

Sometimes I feel compelled to chant or vocalize without speaking words, and I understand that self expression serves to balance my energy.

Teaching and bringing enlightenment to others is a fulfilling practice, even if in small or informal settings.

I am aligned with my highest truth, and I communicate all my needs with love, understanding, and empathy.

I recognize the importance of sharing insight with others, and am confident in my ability to relay ideas accurately.

My truth is an integral piece in the tapestry of voices in the world, and sharing it only helps complete the picture.

When my truth is spoken, it shines a light on things that can only be seen when I speak.

In confidently expressing myself, it helps others feel safe in expressing themselves as well.

In this day and age, I recognize that truth is more important to express than ever, and I am willing to speak my truth more often.

When others react in anger to something I've said, it is because my own truth has exposed an unhealed aspect of their psyche.

I am able to stand in confidence with myself through my voice, and I use my voice to establish my presence with others in a physical setting.

My voice represents the vibrational signature of my identity, and I am grateful for those who appreciate its sound.

Freedom of speech is as much a democratic right as it is an individual one, and I exercise this ethical right with authority.

When I speak, I cut through the old, stagnant belief systems others are stubbornly holding onto.

I look forward to finding opportunities to express my voice.

I recognize the value of intrapersonal expression, such as journaling, writing poetry and creating music.

I feel safe and invigorated in my ability to express myself.

I can feel my throat chakra expanding as it incorporates the energy of my heart and lower chakras, rotating at a healthy diameter.

As I regularly balance my chakras, I will be capable of expressing higher abstract thought, insight, and compassion through my throat chakra.

SIXTH, THIRD EYE CHAKRA

I am willing to receive spiritual insight that I am ready for but have resisted until now.

I am confident that my system is capable of perceiving spiritual information without feeling overwhelmed or scared.

I trust my intuition to guide each of my decisions.

I understand that truth, while simple, can also be complex, and my inner sight will help me discern what is most relevant for me to know at a given time.

Mental clarity is like water in a pond that is clearly seen

through once its debris has settled. With this in mind, I will make a daily effort to still and clear my mind of mental debris, so that greater clarity in my thoughts is achieved.

My third eye has been with me for my entire life, and it continues to provide subtle insights which guide my decisions.

I am ready for the subtle communications and insights of my third eye, which have been provided to me for my entire life, to grow in clarity and frequency.

Being able to receive inner sight is a gift, and I hold this ability with great respect.

The way that spirit communicates with me is varied, but sometimes it is through imagery and symbols that help me better understand a situation.

When I clear my mind and ask that only that information which serves my highest good be transmitted, I can be confident the impressions I receive are in my best interest.

I am open to working constructively with this ability to receive information in my daily life.

I can trust my own psychic safety by setting a positive intent.

I use my inner sight, or imagination to envision the positive outcome of different situations in life.

The images I receive can be used as inspiration for a project, or direction in helping myself heal.

My perception and understanding of the world is always expanding.

Visualization is a powerful tool to create the goals I work toward, and I use this tool in different areas of my life.

I enjoy uncovering the subtle truths of life.

I have the active intention to psychically engage only with entities who are interested in my benefit.

Meditation and focus on my inner sight is an effective way to develop my third eye sensitivity, and I will engage in this practice regularly.

My third eye is becoming clearer every day, and often

shows me inspiration and guidance from my higher self.

I can ask for clarification from the universe, or the source of an image for what a given piece of information represents.

I am open to the ways the universe wants to help me grow through my third eye, and I have faith in my own process to guide me safely.

My third eye is a powerful way to connect psychically with others, and I will use this ability in the interest of service and compassion.

Developing inner sight is also about cultivating inner awareness, and I will achieve this by maintaining a mindful attitude.

If I am feeling overwhelmed by information coming in through my third eye, I can request that my third eye be protected, and only let in information relevant to me achieving balance.

The inspiration and visions that come through my third eye can be used to build systems of prosperity for myself, and I am open to receiving information about this prospect.

I recognize that by going outside my comfort zone, I can more easily find balance within myself.

Developing my intuition is a central interest of my life, and patiently working with my third eye will facilitate this experience.

Visualization is a powerful tool for manifesting, and I will endeavor to use it only for positive means.

I am always growing, and my third eye serves as a headlight that shows the way through the dark.

Like my other chakras, my third eye seeks to serve me and my highest good, and I express my gratitude to it for this service.

In evaluating past experiences, I can extract any lessons that I might have missed, and move on in confidence.

I am open to receiving input from my guides, at appropriate times in whatever format is most relevant.

My third eye, when properly open, prevents me from encountering obstacles and difficult situations I might have otherwise not avoided.

My third eye chakra helps make life fun, as it fuels the visions for my creations, both in work and play.

Some information which enters through my third eye may not be in my best interest, and if I sense this is the case, I can ask that it be dismissed.

I will strive to exercise discernment in life, with all sources of information which present themselves to me.

My inner eye only shows me things I am ready to see, so even if I see something unpleasant, I know I can handle it.

The clearest inner sight is achieved from knowing yourself intimately, and I will strive to better understand my true feelings to develop this clarity.

I look for the interconnectedness between people, and this tendency helps me better serve the world.

I am willing to face the dark aspects of myself, and my past, in order to heal and move on in life.

I turn my dreams into reality.

I can feel my third eye chakra gently rotating in synchronization with its adjacent chakras.

SEVENTH, CROWN CHAKRA

I am one in mind, body and spirit.

I am one with life on this planet.

I am one with the totality of existence.

I am capable of synthesizing complex systems of information, and my crown chakra is perfectly equipped for the job.

I am willing to do the work on myself to make room for the higher insight available to me.

I am willing to receive higher guidance from the universe in whatever form it may take.

My crown chakra is open safely, and is willing to receive all benevolent forms of information that is beneficial for my life.

The universe contains all information, and this information can be understood and experienced.

I am a capable and powerful conduit through which the universe expresses spiritual truth.

When the time comes, I will be willing to educate and inform others of the wisdom I have gained on my path.

The universe seeks to unify all discordance and chaos into harmony.

In seeking to unify the chaos and disharmony in my life, the universe actively works to support me.

I am deserving and capable of healing detrimental, expired systems of thought which no longer serve me.

I am ready to release negative and damaging beliefs which no longer serve my growth or highest good.

In letting go of old thought forms, it also helps others

in my proximity release similar beliefs standing in
their way.

I am excited to reorient my thinking to more
harmonious, inclusive thoughts which incorporate the
broader picture.

I find joy in acting out of spiritual alignment, knowing
that in doing so it sets an example for others.

I will look to integrate universal wisdom with humility,
knowing I am not above or below anyone else.

Making sense of a complex picture takes time, and I
accept that the information I receive will sometimes
appear abstract and confusing.

Even though I may gain access to greater spiritual
understanding, this does not make me a better person
than those around me.

I will avoid the pitfalls of spiritual ego by intending to
use the insights I gain only to help others.

Existence is a process of spiritual evolution, and the
wisdom gained through each lesson makes room for
wisdom of similar logic.

I am complete in my imperfection.

I act with holistic intent to heal and serve the world where I am guided.

Through calming my mind and regular meditation, I will cultivate the ideal conditions for receiving higher information.

Through finding balance in thought, emotion, and action, I can achieve higher perspective and I am grateful for the tools I have at my disposal for supporting this.

I am open to unconventional experiences which will help me grow, that might fall outside my realm of expectation.

There is a higher system of organization in my life, and this system serves my highest good.

The universe has a wealth of information to share with me, and it is best received when my mind is open and at peace.

I am fascinated by the mysteries of the universe, and will continue to pursue them with positive intent.

I will make more time for myself to relax my mind, and keep my crown chakra open to receive relevant information to my path.

I am open to receiving higher inspiration in abstract form, knowing that its meaning will eventually make itself clear to me.

I exercise mastery over my thoughts, and the energy I cultivate with my intentions.

I understand that in exercising mastery over my thoughts, I become a more powerful co-creator in my reality.

I am always manifesting, but my manifestations become more significant when I exercise disciplined intent with my thoughts.

The more I have a thought, the more I create that experience in my reality. As a result, I will focus on thoughts that are expansive and healing.

At any given time, there is a universal mystery waiting to make itself known to me.

When I am aligned and in balance, I am a powerful

teacher through which higher dimensional truth expresses itself.

I am fascinated by the variety of experience the universe yields, and I seek to understand the underlying wisdom shared between these experiences.

I am willing to let go of dated, and expired beliefs which no longer serve me, despite how difficult it may be to do so.

I am willing to yield to my highest truths, in whatever form they may take, so that I can experience greater insight and fulfillment in my life.

My crown chakra is rotating confidently and unobstructed.

CLOSING AFFIRMATIONS

I am loved, whole, and radiantly shining on all levels of self.

I hold compassion for myself, even the parts I haven't yet accepted.

I am a worthy, beautiful being, and knowledge of this fact reinforces my mental, emotional, and energetic health.

I am grounded to the planet, and connected to the higher realms in joy, peace, and compassion.

I am full of light, love, and power, and I willingly share these energies with the world.

Each of my seven chakras are rotating in alignment with each other, in unison and with ease.

CONCLUSION

Wonderful work! I would encourage you to take a minute or sit in quiet, as the energy work from this session will continue to take effect as long as the intention of these affirmations is held. As noted before, each affirmation contained is energetically tailored to heal, balance, and release a spectrum of issues associated with each chakra.

Because these affirmations are designed for repeated use, I would highly encourage you to return to them whenever you are feeling lost, worried, or out of balance. Given the dynamic nature of our personal evolution, one affirmation may hold greater potency for you at a given time than another, so whenever you feel compelled to return to a given chakra, listen to your intuition.

In truth, you wouldn't be here on this planet, seeking this information if you weren't an inspiring, capable and loving powerhouse. So please, take heart in your own heart, love yourself, and keep opening to healing. You're already doing a wonderful job.

Thank you eternally,

Asa

Made in United States
Orlando, FL
22 February 2022

15069161R00037